I0772690

Coloring book for adults
35 amazing dragon
Stress Relieving Designs
Relaxation

This coloring book is belongs to

____

____

____

www.ingramcontent.com/pod-product-compliance
Lightning Source LLC
Chambersburg PA
CBHW081318250726
48662CB00008B/2641